Love is What Love Does!

ISBN: 978-0-578-98953-2
Distributed by Power Of Purpose Publishing
Www.PopPublishing.com
Atlanta, Ga. 30326

Table of Contents

Introduction

This book is targeted to anyone who's battled with the word love. People use the word love so freely. So many people say I love you but don't show up or put actions behind their verbal approach. This book shares how the author experienced life in many different ways that led to self discovery and finding out what love really meant. Through the journey she has taken, she would like to assist others along their journey to heal broken relationships with people and themselves.

Dedication

Understanding love and how it should be reciprocated was learned from many relationships in my life, whether the relationship was impactful through being sustainable or short lived that brought a lesson. My ancestors and God have carried me and will continue to carry me along my journey and that I'm forever grateful for.

Being a mother was the best thing that has taught me what love is. I dedicate this book to my daughter Tyra Hightower. I hope if you're ever faced with any adversity; you can use the tools that I've taught you to get through life. Your Mommy loves you immensely and that will never change. You're my one and only birth child.

To my sister-child, Nika; you're one of a kind. Seeing you endure the loss of both of your parents (your mom and our dad) has made you resilient. I know you want to experience life on your own, just know I will forever have your back. You're stronger than you know.

To my sunshine, Jeremiah; I've known you since you were 5 and you are my silly chocolate lover birthday twin. I know this past year was hard for you but I promise to be the role of a mother you've always had. I love you Son and we will always be family. You and Tyra are going to be two successful individuals no matter the adversity that comes your way.

To my Spouse, Alicia Brown, thank you for being YOU. You've pushed me and supported me throughout this journey so thank you. We've been on this roller coaster together for some time and you've seen first hand some of the struggles and successes. Losing your mom along this journey was difficult for the both of us, but she encouraged me to be the best Life Coach and to share my life. So this is just the beginning. I love you forever for pushing me even when you didn't have the capacity to do so.

I have one supporter, since we met 11 years ago we instantly connected. My sister-in-love Cherish, I know if you were free, you would support me in the physical but because I'm able to share this and you're able to read this means the world to me. I know you can't wait to get out but use this time to learn YOU. So when you get out, you won't settle for anything. I love you sis!!

To my family, friends and frenemies; thank you all for pushing me and doubting me because your prayers whether it was good or bad gave me the endurance to keep going. I would also like to apologize to anyone who has ever crossed my path and never understood me. During that time I was probably trying to understand who I was. So thank you! Always choose to see light in people instead of darkness because you will never know everything they're going through.

Lastly, I would like to thank Jocelyn. You did it! I shared intimate and vulnerable parts about me to the world to encourage others to get through any circumstance that may come their way. I want to thank Me for never giving up even when I thought it was over. You have never allowed your past mistakes to define you. You have gone through obstacles with a smile on your face but you continue to push. Keep conquering, keep being honest and true to yourself; You're a true diamond in the rough! Losing people through grief became a normal thing but hard to accept because the ones who were your supporters, left before they could see you fly. So keep flying high like the eagle that you are.

Chapter 1

At birth it's very cliche to say it's love at first sight. Many women don't experience love at first sight because of what's led up to having their baby or how the baby got here.

The first stare a baby experiences is their mother or father after the nurse hands them over.. The infant instantly adapts to their mother's voice and smell, even if she herself is not prepared for the job itself.

Pregnancy is a time where the father and mother bond as they prepare for something they created. During pregnancy you can see red flags of how the other person may act, but you ignore them hoping for the best.

Sixteen years ago I was married and pregnant. My pregnancy was pretty normal. No major issues until one day I went to the doctor and they said I gained 20lbs in one week. That's abnormal being that I had just entered my third trimester. The lady told me if I kept gaining weight to contact them. My blood pressure and everything was ok. Three days later it felt like someone was pressing the fast forward button because everything happened very fast. I remember riding with my husband at the time to San Antonio, Texas. Going to the restroom is frequent when pregnant. However, my restroom breaks were more frequent than normal. It got to the point my husband handed me a cup saying he was not going to stop. Lol. So I would go to the back of the truck and use it. Disgusting right. Well he had to deliver the load on time. It's not simple pulling over in an 18 wheeler to use the restroom every hour. I noticed I couldn't get out of the truck without assistance once we made it to our destination. I was deep in my thoughts not wanting to scare him, but I felt like something wasn't right. We headed back to Atlanta the next day. I had on a skirt and noticed the imprint on my thighs. It looked as if my skirt was smothering my thighs. I asked him if he noticed what I saw and he said yes, with a sound of concern in his voice. He immediately asked how I felt. I said outside of peeing I'm ok. But I feel like I'm fat like professor clumps. Before pregnancy I was 135lbs. As we traveled through Louisiana I began to feel extremely exhausted. Just tired; I couldn't keep my eyes open. I would notice him staring at me while he was driving. He was more concerned than me. I then looked in the mirror and my face looked like a different person, I didn't recognize myself. Immediately I began to stress. I knew then I needed to go to the hospital. I told him I think I need to go and his question was, what if they keep you?

The fear of being in another state not around family really scared me. So I held on for another 8 hours. I remember just praying to God to protect me and my baby. We got to his job finally. He assisted me in getting in the car. At this time I looked like a sumo wrestler. We got to the hospital which was literally 2 miles from his job. The lady at registration immediately took me back because she thought I was in labor. But I told her I'm just 7 months pregnant today. My body was exhausted and in excruciating pain because it had been stretched. I stepped on the scale and I had gained a total of 100lbs. The doctor said my numbers were normal and I looked great. But my weight was 100lbs more than what I weighed a week ago. How do I look great? I feel awful and something is not right.

How do I look great?

The doctor said "well, we will keep you overnight for observations." They gave me something for pain in my IV and I was able to rest. They were able to monitor my baby. The next day came and my husband left for work. My Ob-gyn walked in the room and cleared me to go home because everything was normal. I didn't feel good but he's the doctor so who am I? As he was leaving the room, I jumped up saying I peed on myself. He turned around to check. He said wow your water just broke. My numbers changed instantly. My blood pressure went to stroke level and I went in and out. I remember my aunt calling my husband to come back, but he said he was already at work. They said that I would have to go into an emergency c section. I went from being fine to fighting for our lives in the matter of seconds.

Going into surgery I was in and out. I could hear things but couldn't physically see. I heard the doctor saying we have a baby girl and she was crying.

I could also hear my Aunt Screaming and praising God in the midst of the storm. She was saying Thank you Jesus!! Thank you Jesus!!!

This is all I remember about the day of my daughter's birth. I woke up about 1 a.m. grabbing my belly thinking it was all a dream. And it was not. I broke down in tears. Terrified in the hospital alone. I've never been in a hospital overnight and I was alone. With tears going down my face, the nurse came into the room and asked if I was ok. I said yes but I didn't remember having my baby. I thought everything was a dream.

She said yes your baby is downstairs. I asked "when can I see her?" She wheeled me downstairs into a room where my baby was in a see through box with shades on. She looked like a baby alien to me. She was as tiny as my wrist. Tears rolling down my face. The nurse said it's ok. I said that's not my baby. I was too big for her to be so little and "why did she have to look like ET".

The nurse ignored me and said, "she will be fine now, what's your baby's name?" I said Tyra Jade Hightower. She was born 1 lb 12 ozs on 6/15 at 6;18 pm. I couldn't hold her yet because she had to be in the incubator. The doctor came into the room and said I had a feisty baby. The nurse said "sure do, she's not even a day old and running us crazy." Her name will be Feisty Tyra. She then whispered in my ear God has you, everything will be ok.

As I went back to my room I called my husband to see where he was. Of course he was still at work. I felt so alone. Emotions immediately raised in my head. Like how do you leave your wife who is in the hospital to go to work and then I have the baby and you're still not here? How can you say you love me? The next evening about 7 p.m. he walks in with a room full of people. So you passed the hospital and went to go get people before even seeing your wife or your daughter? You don't even know what's going on with either one of us. This is when the anger started. Spending most days in the hospital alone I couldn't go home because the swelling and my blood pressure wouldn't go down. Having a baby unexpectedly, I wasn't prepared. I had to send him to the store called Motherhood for bras because I went from a size 34A to a 36C cup and my breasts were filled with milk. They were so pretty but hurt like hell. My milk produced immediately so pumping was my option.

They don't tell you about the painful stuff when having a baby. I'm here to tell you all that having birth is like life itself. People discuss the beauty of having a baby but never really disclose the struggles of having a baby.

The day I was released it felt awkward because my baby had to stay. I cried. I understood but why me? Why couldn't I have a healthy baby? Why I couldn't carry her full term. Why do I feel

8

so lost? I have to go home and I can't drive for two weeks so how am I going to see my baby because her daddy has to work and I need to see her? I got rides when he was at work, and on his off days he took me to see her. Some mornings I felt like I just wanted to stay in bed, but I knew I had her waiting on me. After a few days they removed her shades and she was able to open her eyes and do skin to skin. That was the best feeling ever. To love someone that will love me with no judgment made me feel like motherhood was worth it. This is love!!

A month passed by and everything was going great until she got fussy and they said she had an infection that could cause her to be brain dead. I remember standing in the hospital hallway talking to the doctor and I just blacked out while he was saying she would not survive, if she lived she would have deformities. I walked away and held my baby while tears rolled down my face. Her Dad was just there; he never said a word. A word of encouragement, no emotion, no nothing. He was just disconnected!

I would go every single day and pray over my baby. The infection required us to wear hazmat suits to go in her room. I didn't care about anything, I wanted to see my baby. She was growing despite the odds ahead of her. She started to get better and the doctor couldn't explain how. I knew God but seeing my baby come through made me believe God even more.

I loved this little human I created but I can't lie and say I didn't know if I was coming or going. I lived 38 miles from the hospital. I would go to the hospital every single day 2- 3 times a day. Sometimes more. I was very hands on with her feedings and anything they had to do with her in the NICU. I was so involved that all the nursing staff knew me. I would see other mothers cry because they had to leave their baby for a day or two. They would treat the nursing staff so rudely because they were emotional and didn't understand why they were discharged but their baby wasn't. I began to encourage them by letting them know other people were in worse situations than them. At least they had a discharge date when some of us didn't know if we were coming or going. Plus Her dad would have to drive by the hospital every day to get to work and to go home, and never stopped by himself. He only would see her if he went with me which was rare, but never by himself. It was so little the nursing staff questioned if he was the father in the beginning. I knew that we both were going through different emotions but I felt so alone. After 2 and a half months in NICU; Tyra beat the odds. She came home with two monitors, an oxygen machine and an apnea machine. This is the part of love no one tells you about. I had to find gratitude in just her being home but the questions and eyes I got whenever we went somewhere. People are so cruel even to babies but I didn't care, I would be ready to snap if I saw a funny face. This process sucks. I still had to smile and act strong but internally I was depleting. I was confused like damn, everyone has healthy babies why not me? I'm glad she's home but now I'm a new mom and a nurse. A nurse to someone who can't tell me when something is wrong and the machines will just go off at random times of the day. No one ever asked how I was mentally at that time. I didn't even think it was a thing.

Chapter 2

Home for only 30 days; I was staring at her. She just looked weird to me. I told her dad I wanted to take her to the ER. I didn't know why, but once they took us to the back she died in front of us. Cold blue is all I heard the nurse scream as they pushed us out the room. Not knowing what was going on I just started to pray, but at this time I was doubting God because he just kept taking me through it. I didn't understand why. She was revived and placed on oxygen. Test after test, day after day I was still there. Of course her dad went to work as usual. He would come up there but not as often as I wanted. We had our own room and yea at that point I figured he had checked out. I didn't understand how he could not show us love during this time or just support. I knew our bills would not stop if he stayed but at least give more effort in just showing up when you're off. That was something he lacked. I felt like he was angry with me for having a sick child as I was angry with myself. She had to have surgery and her dad went to work. I really felt like he just didn't care. During this time at Egleston Children's Hospital I saw other parents suffering like me. I learned some and saw some lose their children. I would always wonder if I was next. However, I found strength, encouraging parents on every floor. I would pray and talk about God and how good he was even in the middle of me doubting him.

Tyra finally made it. My marriage was never the same. I resented him. I hated him. I went back to work and would go to doctor visit after doctor visit and he never went to one. He never even went to the hospital while I was pregnant. I was a single married woman!!! Sometimes I couldn't get out of bed. I just felt stuck. I would make sure my baby was good, Cook, clean and everything in between like a wife should do. Every day I would feel trapped. My husband would entertain the baby and not say a thing to me. What did I do? I made excuses for his negative behavior and said oh that's just him. He's shy and not a talkative person. Our wedding anniversary came and he didn't come home until after midnight. I had cooked this fabulous dinner and he didn't come home or say happy anniversary. I'd had enough. He went to work and I packed my shit and never went back. I couldn't be with someone who couldn't respect me or value me as such. He tried to fight for our relationship months later and I allowed him to manipulate me into working it out. Something in my head just switched and I said fuck this shit!! I will not allow my daughter to see her mom just married and not fucking happy. This is not fucking love!! Love is what love does!!

I knew walking away would be hard but I didn't take the time to think things through because I wanted peace, something I have never experienced mentally. I began to hate him. He doesn't understand anything I went through to bring this child into this world and as a new mother having a sick baby, I was depressed. I didn't like myself and the space I was in. I went from having everything I wanted to having nothing.

One thing I know is that while growing up, love was there but it was incidents that I knew what love was not. Of course growing up in a Christian household I had to learn that love is patient, love is kind, it does not envy or boast.

Well in my household it wasn't always love. Growing up I experienced dysfunction being normalized and because it was normal that was considered love. However, a part of me always knew that love was work but this was not it.

I moved in with my mother which I hated to do because the relationship has always been inconsistent since I was kid. Living there was helpful for my child but not for me. She's an amazing grandmother, but when it comes to me I've never seen the actions of love as she expresses it. Well you know we all have skeletons in our closets. I'm not afraid to now discuss triggers after trigger. She would make me feel guilty for speaking my truth and how experiences have hurt me. She would want me to act as if it didn't happen. She's the master of sweeping things under the rug without holding people accountable. So I was always misunderstood.

I was called stupid for leaving my ex husband because everyone said oh he loved you and treated you great, but I knew I wanted more; I just didn't know what more was. I ended up being a single mother, homeless and jobless with a sick baby. During this time I was making irrational decisions because I was running. But I knew I didn't want to be singly-married any longer. Day in and day out I would feel useless and not worthy, wanted or loved. I couldn't live for anyone else's happiness. I broke his heart because I loved him but not enough because I knew I loved myself more. Through all of this I still didn't know depression was riding my back. What's that? At least 2 years of continuous failures

I just couldn't catch a break. Finding out I was pregnant with a 3 year old I was struggling; because her dad wasn't consistent in taking care of her. Also I made an irrational decision just for my happiness. I walked away from an amazing man. He loved me, he would do anything for me, provided financially but showed up unavailable emotionally, socially, verbally and mentally. But this is not about him it's about ME!

What should I expect from a person who wasn't there during my pregnancy? No it wasn't his kid. We had been broken up for almost 2 years but he wouldn't file so I filed for a divorce. He showed no interest in showing up to court.

I was dating a guy and found myself pregnant.

Questioning God because I just kept going through.

I found myself going out all the time and drinking heavily, but I would wake up to the same problems or more.

After knowing that I was pregnant knowing that I've never wanted to be a single mother of one, but now this would be two. I thought I was careful but I guess it was a drunken night. I cried and cried. I tried to kill myself. I wanted out!! I lost it! I felt like the whole world was on my back and shit after shit was just piling up on me. I was over it.

I became a walking zombie and I chose DEATH!!! From actually driving on a highway of high speed wanting to die. Attempting to do physical harm to my body.

One day I just snapped. I wanted out. The thoughts of me being dead sounded so easy to me. After days of doing things like taking pills and feeling restless I finally told my family I wanted out. They thought this was the day I chose not to live. It wasn't, this was the night I had a revelation as my family prayed over me during my mental breakdown.

I was so caught up into the normality of dysfunction that I didn't know what normal felt like.

I kept saying in my head the people that's praying for me are the most crooked Christians contributing to my unhappiness.

During my breakdown I could see the flaws in everyone including myself.

What do you do when not one single person is authentic in your life? Everyone only wants to be around you for their benefit. I was alone. I didn't know how to express my feelings. Whenever I said I didn't feel right the response was "give it to God". How could I give it to God when I was told he sees all. If I'm his child, why does he have me suffering like this? I just wanted to be happy and strong for my daughter. I was so weak I couldn't see past what I was going through.

Has someone ever dismissed your feelings? How did you deal or did you just act as if it didn't happen? Not being true to your feelings can contribute to a trigger of your depression you may feel. So now instead of you dealing with it you're now becoming a contributing factor of why you feel the way you are. I had to be free from my own thoughts. Use this space to release things you've been just sweeping under the rug and not addressing because you don't want to end up like me. So keep going!!

_____

_____

_____

_____

_____

Chapter 3

I slept through the night and woke up choosing life over my circumstances. I sat outside still mad at the world, but knew there should be more to this. Something just clicked in me. I had to choose life because I knew in my heart the people who were praying for me; I didn't want them raising my child; That was my fuel. I didn't know my purpose but I do know every person I encountered over my life I helped without expecting anything in return. I did know I treated people how I desired to be treated but no one ever treated me the same. Not even the ones who I opened my heart to or my legs for.

I made a hair appointment and cut my hair. I started working out. I woke up everyday saying that I will choose ME everyday for the rest of my life. I will no longer be my circumstances. This is the day I didn't know anything about affirmations or ever wanted to read up on it, but something in me gave me the power.

They say when a woman cuts her hair, she's in revolution to start something new. I began to love me and love my child even more because she's my reason, but I didn't know my purpose. One thing I did know is that I had a gift. I had a gift of helping people. I wanted more out of life. I left my ex because I felt trapped and vowed to myself not to be married to someone who will make me feel stuck. Stuck in their habits and lose myself where I can't be the leader and eagle I was destined to be. Here I am sitting here trapped in my own thoughts. I'm expecting people to love me unconditionally but I'm not loving myself.

The things I didn't know about motherhood and marriage, until I actually experienced my own journey, because everyone's story is not the same. Some people have multiple children, natural birth and no health issues. Whereas, some can't say the same. Your journey is custom made for you. Either your journey will make you stronger or you will have continuous lessons until you reach your destiny. At 22 years old I didn't know if I was coming or going but I knew I was destined for greatness, if I stayed the course. I knew at times I wanted to give up but something in me kept saying you got this girl. I didn't know what kept pushing me because I felt so heavy. Many people didn't know I was in a dark place because I faked a smile. But my inside was dark. I didn't treat people how I felt but I knew I needed to do some work.

A month later I signed up for college. After sitting and trying to find my purpose I knew I wanted to help people but didn't know how. So, I signed up for college and after talking to my advisor she said to try Human Services. Human Services is a background of psychology. Class after class after class I began to learn. One day my instructor said you would be required to go to counseling, so that you will know how to counsel.

Faking it until I made it was a generational curse that was instilled in me as a kid. My family would act as if they had a certain status and people would assume that we did because we dressed up to par. Not knowing the daily struggles. One thing my mom would always say was, "never look like what you're going through. "That has always been in my head, however I think it's important to look in the mirror and acknowledge what you're going through so you can grow through it. Acting as if it's not there can ultimately harm you mentally, and that will lead to other damage, affecting how you deal with people, especially how you treat them.

Not addressing your flaws will make you the 'mean person' because you begin to make yourself feel good for tearing down

17

others. It can then affect receiving the love others have for you, because you internally don't know your value. So you sabotage what's in front of you, whether it's a genuine friendship or an intimate relationship because YOU don't believe you're worthy. So I challenge you to look in the mirror every week, and work towards becoming a better version of you to love so that you can receive love in an authentic way.

Understanding that it's ok to Not be ok.

The thoughts of suicide when feeling overwhelmed and or depressed is very common. Many people aren't honest about this because they feel it's a demonic spirit that's talking over the person's thoughts, but in reality it's the person that's just burned out with racing mentally, physically, emotionally, socially and financially. When you're just overwhelmed because the world feels like it's on your shoulders and you have no way out. During this time, you feel no one understands. Suicidal ideation does not have a look of a person. Anyone can experience this no matter the financial status or perceived life that the public visualizes.

It's ok to not feel ok.

Acknowledge your feelings.

If you're having suicidal thoughts, please ask for help. You can't be the best version of yourself if you don't believe in yourself, trust yourself or trust the process. It's a choice to move forward although the road may give you obstacles.

You must choose but if you need help: Contact the national suicide hot line for assistance 1-800-273-8255.

Find someone you trust that you can speak with.

Chapter 4

They say get married, have children and have a career. They don't tell you the in- between. They don't tell you about the process and how life can kick you in the ass and feeling sad is normal. They don't tell you things prior to getting married and having a child is a part of your journey and makes you who you are along the way. It's up to you to heal.

Everyone will experience some type of trauma over their life whether it's death, a breakup, family turmoil and or illness or things out of your control. As I peel back the scab off each scar I must peel back one of my biggest scars.

Prior to having my daughter, I grew up without my father physically being inconsistent, but provided what child support ordered financially. Whatever he and my mother had going on hindered us from having a consistent relationship until I turned 13 and was able to have my own relationship with him. Experiencing the hate between the two; I always said if I had a child they would never see me act crazy or speak negatively about their father. We developed an amazing relationship that was cut short.

My Dad passed away when I was 18 years old; a senior in high school right before Christmas. I had been through some things in my life but this by far took the cake. Grief!! My mom didn't send me to grief counseling or asked if I was ok. At that time I felt like she was happy for his passing. I'm the only child with the two of them together. I'm the oldest of all of my siblings. I have always been the odd ball and felt out of place. No matter what accomplishment or achievement was made I would always hear about what I wasn't. If I ever heard anything good about me, it was used as bragging rights while talking to their friends.

My mom would always say you act just like your dad. My dad had severe anger issues but was the sweetest person on earth. He loved hard but if you messed with him or someone he cared about; he would go for blood. I knew when I got upset I was a replication of my dad. I was "the outspoken" child. If I felt something was unfair I would speak on it and get many whoopings for it. Now that I look back at the mistreatment, it was a controlling tactic used to attempt to "shut me up". They wanted me to think and believe what they wanted, but I wanted something better than what I was experiencing.

Be intentional with your words, your words can be harmful mentally and lead to emotional trauma to a person.

Chapter 5

Going to school and counseling allowed me to peel each layer back. Then I went more on a holistic journey. I learned about shadow work.

So doing my shadow work I had to acknowledge that I was still holding on to my dad and had never grieved him. I acted as if he was away and not dead. I didn't know how to express my feelings.

During school I had to write papers about my feelings and struggles head on. I couldn't run. Peeling each scar one by one and understanding that my foundation was not solid. There were so many weeds at the root of the problem and it all stemmed from my mother.

As I began the healing journey; I learned another scar was the relationship with my mother. She says "I Love you", however the little girl inside of me always shows up and says "well show it". We don't understand unhealed trauma in relationships can cause dysfunction. Especially if one person is seeking healing and the other feels their actions are validated. Love is what love does. Even if you're a spiritual person or just a person who lives by the law of reciprocity; you will understand that you treat others how you want to be treated.

She's painted me to be the bad guy because I've chosen to live fearlessly by speaking on how things have impacted me. I chose to walk unapologetically in my truth about how things in my life have cultivated me to who I am now and becoming. I love my mom because she did her best with what she knew. Having a relationship as a parent and child requires healing or there will be a continuation of generational curses. If you, the parent, are not healed; it can cause trauma for the child growing up and rolling into adulthood. This can affect future relationships. So I had to heal as an adult battling being misunderstood.

Understand no one can tell you how you feel about something. Your feelings are yours and don't need validation of how something has impacted you. One unique thing about us is we all were created differently; Your brain, your fingerprint, the way you look is different from the next person. You may have similarities but no one is the same. Your perspective on life can be something that was instilled in you as a child to help formulate your thinking but it's up to you to broaden your thinking. Do your own research. I noticed things and ways I was taught; I don't teach my child. Not saying I was taught wrong but I was taught a learned behavior from another teacher. The great thing about this life, as you get older and mature you learn your own perspective. It's ok to agree to disagree with others and not be mad. It's not about who is right or wrong. I respect you and expect the same. I thank God everyday for making us different. If we were the same this world would be even more crazy.

Healing is a journey that can't require any judgment.

Hurt people can't heal people but people who acknowledge their brokenness and are willing to do the work can bring light to their darkness.

Going to counseling and acknowledging my shadows was life changing. Shadow work is something everyone should complete because this process allows you to look in the mirror and acknowledge the ugly truth. You learn how and why you act the way you act or move the way you move. I use the tree of life as my business logo because it reminds me of a human. Shadow work requires you to find the root of the problem. You're like a tree. A tree has roots, that's your parents who created you, and their upbringing. Sometimes the root has weeds. The weeds are things that they have carried on as we call them generational curses. Sometimes the weed over powers the growth and can make a person stagnant because of the choices their parents have made. My definition of Shadow work "It hurts looking in the mirror at each scar and remembering how it got there." A tree has many scars from the environment, weather and mistreatment from people. That's why in the middle of the tree there is a broken heart because life will break you. Life is people, places and things because we put expectations on them instead of ourselves.

I've looked at myself as if I was a tree. I'm a force to be reckoned with and it would take a hell of a storm from God himself to knock me out of here now that I know my strength. I may lose some leaves meaning character traits to make me better or even lose some dead branches, that's trumping my growth. I choose to give energy and life to others who respect me, even those who can't stand me because that's the storm and rain. I need the water from the storm to survive. So the doubters and haters are now my fuel to success. Doing shadow work is a different type of healing because you come to grips that how a person feels about you is not your business. If a person is not willing to explain and properly communicate with you how they feel then the problem is not you but them.

During this journey I had to come to grips that I was in severe postpartum depression also dealing with grief I never acknowledged. I made irrational decisions because I was depressed. Depression in African American culture is unheard of, especially in a Christian family. I was a little girl trapped in an adult body looking for validation from my mother. Now I'm a Mother who would rather die than have my child feel the pain I feel on a daily basis. I didn't want my daughter to grow up in dysfunction by staying with her Dad. I also didn't want my daughter to ever feel like I didn't love her. You're told to pray it away. After prayer and prayer, I still wanted to be dead. Sometimes the worst place to be in is in your head. You can have people in your physical presence but unavailable to help you mentally because they're in their own head. This is the stuff people don't tell you about life.

_____

_____

_____

_____

_____

_____

Have you ever felt alone but something in you yearns for love from others? If yes…what did you do to move past seeking validation but establish authentic relationships.

Have you ever just sat with yourself and acknowledged your flaws? Take this time to write them out. Once you see them then write how you can change them to become your BEST SELF? Be vulnerable and honest

25

Chapter 6

Unhealed trauma would cause your mind to perceive things that are not there; especially if the hurt is consistent. In order to heal you will have to stop looking for things that aren't there. Remember, what you eat is the same as what you think. What I've learned about trauma, when it's something normal you've experienced in your life; you don't know the pain it's caused, until you heal. Controlling your thoughts to be positive will allow yourself to receive higher vibrations to manifest light in your life.

Like the old Proverbs say, "Reckless words can pierce your soul but a tongue of the wise brings healing."

If you don't address your childhood traumas your relationships will suffer, especially your intimate relationships.

When the root has so many weeds around it; you will have to treat the weed by going to counseling and pick each weed out by addressing the issues at hand. Having a voice in the African American black household is considered disrespectful. But when are we going to hold everyone accountable and heal the broken families? Trauma can lead to unaddressed hurt that becomes a domino effect of pain you carry. You will walk around wounded and have a hard time building authentic relationships because you attract your hurt. Many people have or will experience some type of grief that can cause depression. Whether the death of a friend, family member, relationship, job or career, or simply yourself can lead to a dark place.

Experiencing grief is sharing your love with someone who is not here to reciprocate the love in return as they used to in the flesh.

Grief is always classified as a feeling that's known to mankind. The response to grief is an experience of sadness, anger, rage, denial, blame. A death is caused when the spirit leaves Its earthly body eternally; however, you can experience grief without a physical death of a person. Experiencing some type of grief will have you saying you're fine on days when you know for a fact; you don't know if you're coming or going. You're stuck on a roller coaster of emotions and don't know when it's over or when your feelings will get to a level ride. If you want change; you must change even through the ugliness. Grief is a very dark place. You experience disbelief which is a numb feeling that can last years. Denial is how I got through my day as long as I acted like a situation didn't happen I was good. I could wake up happy. Pretty much faking it until I made it but I never made it anywhere. I know I'm not the only one that would go through things and just act as if it didn't happen. Except when anger would ride my back. I masked anger so well. I would feel like well maybe if I said this my Dad would be here. If my Dad was here things would be different. As soon as someone pissed me off I would have a range of emotions and couldn't explain where that came from. Asking God why Me? Dang, why am I so upset? Naw girl you tripping is always what I said to myself when I realized I overreacted. As I was in a dark place I would always bargain with God like well, you could've just taken me. Life is so hard. Why do I have to go through this?

As stated before this is not just the physical death of a person. What if I worked more hours they would've appreciated me? Maybe if I would've spent more time with him or her they wouldn't have cheated? Maybe if I went to the doctor sooner I would've known. Maybe if I let them keep disrespecting me they would love me? Maybe if I just didn't say anything they would want me around?

Stop it!!! Because when that happens, that little evil spirit called depression takes over you. You begin to feel heavy, confused and isolated. When people are depressed they're not going to admit it especially if they've never experienced it before.

Hi my name is Jocelyn I'm depressed!

Nooo absolutely not! I didn't know I was depressed until 8 years after my father's death. It took trauma after trauma to keep happening for me to realize I've allowed myself to become a punching bag. I was taking hit after hit. Death of my best friend/Dad, death of relationships with family, friends and even career to look in the mirror and realize it's not the people around me. It's ME! I'm the problem! This was my breaking and awakening after attempting suicide. I had to learn to accept things I couldn't change and to have the courage to change things I could. I had to learn to quit overthinking and replaying failed scenarios in my head. I was feeding the self-doubt, anxiety and seeing the good in everyone but me. . The anxiety was controlling my mind because I didn't have consistency in my corner. Everyone I thought was supposed to be there for me was either dead physically, or fake physically.

The consistency that was not there was me. I had to push myself when I had no energy to do so. Sometimes pushing myself to be around people who are light so they can shine enough on me to give me the energy I need.

Even in your dark days, you gravitate to the light/ energy of others to help you push through.

Have you ever grieved a living being? Grieving a person that's alive is training your brain psychologically not to remember them and the baggage they come with.

People only talk about grief in a good light of missing someone who treated you well. But what about grieving someone who didn't treat you well? Your grief is not the person but you grieve the should of, could of and would of's. The resentment of not having good memories can make this even harder. To understand the difference requires transparency with self.

For example, I know my mom loves me, because she says it, yet I feel her actions are not loving towards me. She doesn't recognize me like she does others or acknowledges the hurtful things she's done to me when my feelings are just as valid as her's. The little girl inside of me would always want validation and protection from her, but she didn't see things from my view. I would always be sad about it, especially knowing I had a daughter. She would see the dysfunction. However, it could all be so simple if love is what love does. Stop saying I love you and do love with actions. Do I sit in a depressed state because our relationship is strained after several attempts I've made to reconcile? Continue to have an on and off again relationship where we don't talk for months or years. At some point in life if the other party is not willing to be accountable for their actions in a situation the best solution is to walk away. Your peace and growth is more important. No relationship whether it's your parents, children, spouse or friends should be one sided. Everyone has feelings and they should be respected and understood that they will not be the same all the time because you are individuals with your own thought process. It's ok to agree to disagree with respect.

These people who you may experience this with, may have a cycle of coming in and out of your life for their benefit. You will get backlash for establishing boundaries because you prefer consistency and respect.

With courage I vowed to change ME. Why did I choose to change myself? Because I can't change anyone else but me and how I respond to someone's actions. I will forever seek the wisdom to know the difference as situations arise because I'm human. I will take accountability for my actions, especially those that affect others and more importantly MYSELF.

At this point you will gradually find things that bring you joy to accept what has happened in your life. I chose to be different and not allow my daughter to be raised by a broken mother but one who is doing her best to heal so that she doesn't have to suffer from my hidden traumas.

Will you have moments where you still grieve situations or a person? Absolutely!

Don't act if it's not there. Feel those emotions, take a deep breath and release.

It's ok not to feel ok! Feel the emotions, acknowledge them, if you can't shake it. Make an appointment to speak to someone to get the help you need.

Going through the loss of my dad made it easy for me to walk away from relationships because I always felt people are only temporary beings anyway. I had no consistency of unconditional love.

Losing my Dad, I've always thought about the what if's?

I got married twice and my dad wasn't there. I've been through some things in my life and I've felt alone. Until I feel a warm presence, then I'm reminded that he has pushed me along this journey of life. Every success and failure he's been with me. It's just hard to swallow the pill of acceptance because grief feels like you just handed someone your heart and you're waiting for them to bring it back but they never do. You feel like a piece of you is gone and it's hard to function because you only have the memories to move forward. Sometimes the memories are good and sometimes they are bad.

Death is one of the guarantees in this life. You live and you die. Some descend sooner than others, but if you're born you will die. We understand that simple thought however, we don't understand the heaviness it brings. Grief is not just a mental pain; it can cause you to not feel your physical presence any longer because you're stuck at the thought of the loss.

Use this time to write the roller coaster of emotions you feel.

_____

_____

_____

_____

_____

_____

Don't stay stuck at the thought of the loss but learn to live through it. Allow yourself to feel then do things to honor the person you're missing or just do something for yourself to honor your push to move past the loss.

Journal intentions and goals of how you could honor yourself for moving past being stuck in the loss.

_____

_____

_____

_____

_____

_____

Chapter 7

Marriage /relationships

Going through my own traumas, I didn't have the capacity to be good to my husband because I wasn't good to myself. Even though I held the house down as a walking zombie, I expected him to be emotionally available to me not realizing he wasn't there for himself. Yes, I went back and apologized to him. Apologizing wasn't something I did to make me feel better but it helped me not go through life with resentment or any hurt towards him. I also value him and always will as my child's father, so loving him in an unconditional way will always be because we made a human together. I had to acknowledge that he had his own unhealed traumas that he's not willing to heal from. This apology isn't for him but for me. He didn't receive it well because he wasn't in a healed space.

Many people can give their opinion on marriage because most people desire being married. Many want the title but are unaware of the work that's required to keep it together. A marriage requires healthy communication, understanding that we're both human and will not always agree but we can agree to disagree; full transparency and commitment to be together whether there is rain or sunshine.

Remember love is what love does so don't say you love your partner without putting in the work to have intimacy. Intimacy is you being into each other mentally, physically, emotionally and sexually. When marriage gets tough; don't give up. Do the work. The work requires transparency through effective communication, listening to hear and not to respond. Sometimes when marriage has hit a pivotal point please look in the mirror individually. The battle in marriage is sometimes a fight between the little girl or little boy inside of you. In a marriage people tend to lose themselves. Sometimes in a marriage you two can be physically present but one or both are in tune with other music. Why? Because it's human nature to go through things individually and not have the capacity to juggle the two. So in a marriage you should be supportive and understanding to prevent the other person from losing themselves. This requires true transparency and selfless acts to make sure that you both are in a good mental space. This is what love is…. When this happens; communicate your wants and needs so they can be elevated. You're going to change during a marriage. Your wants and needs now will be different years later. This is why your ring is a circle. You will repeat things in life but ultimately get better with your response. Once both individuals understand that they are two broken people who want to love through their imperfections perfectly and unconditionally; then there could be sustainability in relationships. Many people go into relationships feeling as though they've succeeded with everything except marriage, then once they're married it becomes rocky. Marriage begins to expose who they really are.

When sickness, loss of employment, or grief enters the marriage it can change the dynamics of the marriage and how each view of the other is.

There are a few views of a marriage during hardship. The one who may think they're doing everything. Then the one who feels like they're trying but it's never enough.

The third view is your vows but your ego forgets those when tough times arise. Majority of people vow through sickness, health, richer or poor. But as soon as things turn sour they run or feel uncomfortable they move around. In a marriage, transition will happen especially if you plan to be married for 10 or more years. So you can't just get married off of the hype, lust or just love alone. Sometimes when you're in love you disregard the red flags of who the person really is. During the honeymoon phase of the marriage, everything is great; then reality hits. Life becomes routine, then kids or issues come along the way that requires your focus not being solely into each other.

You can lose your identity in a marriage or relationship. How do you know you've lost your identity? I've lost my identity in a marriage and relationship because I'm a natural caregiver and nurturer. I would forget what I like, my sense of purpose, my peace, wants and sometimes needs. It wasn't intentional. I'm just a natural solver. I like to fix things that I can. But when I looked in the mirror I was unhappy and I couldn't be mad at anyone but ME. I had to become intentional with my self happiness as I was intentional on making everyone else happy. When you're intentional with who you are. You're able to see and identify things that aren't bringing value to you. So you now see that you've become so routine enjoying the idea of family but dodging the disrespect because of comfort. You've become complacent with everything.

So here you are thinking you're good and you've won the jackpot. Yes, you had all your amenities on display, the other person thought you were fine. You're taking pictures all on social media saying #relationshipgoals. As soon as a disagreement happens and you've triggered something from the past, they raise their voice. You then say he or she is toxic. They're narcissistic! They're manipulative! They're gaslighting you! Picking arguments brings you out of character and now you think there's something wrong with you. You're now grieving over a good time with a person who you felt was the one. Not knowing you both may have grown up in two different households and the communication tactics were different so now we have to teach each other how we're going to communicate in this new relationship. You then establish healthy boundaries. When learning someone they're not going to immediately peel back all of their traumas they've experienced. Why? Because being vulnerable requires another level of trust. However, understanding your trauma triggers is something everyone should learn for themselves, that love is what love does. This will help in all relationships. Once you're good to yourself, you will be able to serve others in a better capacity.

Often times people will end friendships because they say 'it's draining or we're not married.' Friendships are similar to a marriage except you don't have sexual relations with them, pay bills or are required to talk to them daily.

However, a lot of friendships end because one is giving more than the other. One is always available as the other is only available when they have something going on that needs to be addressed. Just like a marriage, you should have intentions on building friendships that are equally yoked for your life and success. Everyone is not your friend but use the term so lightly. It requires transparency and vulnerability just like a marriage. You can't have true friends and they don't know when you're happy or sad. Who wants to be friends with a wall? You're only here for the turn up; people can lean on you , dance on you but you have no emotions when someone punches a hole in you, kicks you or falls on you.

Love is what love does! Many people don't understand the dynamics of how you communicate with others whether it's family or friends. Not knowing it will follow and roll onto your kids. As adults we must break the generational curses by allowing ourselves to be more vulnerable than how we were taught. In this day and time, our children are exposed to many avenues that show them how to feel. So you who's reading this, let's ask yourself; Is love really what love does? Does the little girl and little boy inside of you seek validation, especially the ones who lack the attention from their parents or loved ones? Acknowledging the little girl or little boy inside of you is important before communicating with others. It will help you understand why you choose different relationships. I sought friendships to create a family because the little girl inside of me had always felt rejected and neglected by my family. So, I value friendship. This is an example of how you evaluate and examine your life to help you heal your childhood hurt.

1. Talk to the little person in you. Apologize to her/him for holding on to traumas that's allowing you to make proper adult decisions because you're protecting them. Hurt people hurt people but before they hurt people they hurt themselves. Stop hurting you!!!

2. If you want to have authentic relationships with family, friends and even your spouse; stop neglecting you. Healing your traumas that you've experienced as a kid into adulthood is not an easy task but it's worth it. If you value yourself; you will do the work. If you don't know your worth; I'm here to teach.

This will help not only you but any relationship you encounter. To have successful relationships requires authenticity, accountability and constant forgiveness.

Authenticity is knowing and showing your true self behind the things you try to mask.

Accountability is having an understanding that no one is perfect, not even you. Having the ability to apologize when you've wronged someone.

Forgiveness is being able to let things go. Process the hurt by acknowledging your feelings. Forgiveness does NOT mean you're condoning any disrespectful behavior. It means you've acknowledged the problem and you choose not to hold grudges, build resentment or vengeance.

3. Lastly, remembering that you will grow throughout relationships and sometimes you will fall out of love, but if you have the foundation of just loving their presence and liking who they are, you will get past the growth process. Once the love and like is gone; evaluate if you are just now codependent because you've become complacent. This is a journey that's never ending because our wants and needs change as we grow.

First thing you need to do is forgive yourself!!!!! Then write things you may be holding onto.

_____

_____

_____

_____

_____

_____

What is the little girl or little boy inside of you seeking? Mine was validation that I'm loved because I felt abandoned. So understanding this about myself, I had to acknowledge when certain situations happened. It's not that serious, it triggered something inside of me that needs healing. I love to feel wanted. So acknowledging why I desire to be wanted or needed is important to me.

I used an example to show you how I understand my triggers from the little girl inside of me. Share what triggers you......

Chapter 8

Many people grow up in households with parents who have some type of an addiction. Addictions can be to careers, food, drug, alcohol, video games, women and or men just to name a few. As the children who are raised by these parents they grow up with some type of resentment or anger. As a functioning adult who has had a parent with an addiction it always feels like you're in competition with the addiction. As long as the person is still addicted it's hard to build a relationship because you're expecting them to respond the way you want. However, you as a sober person will have to meet them where they are. Although it is traumatic for you, there is a weed holding them to that addiction. Something they're hiding that's driving them to a numbing state so they're reality is altered.

When building a relationship with an addict you must first stop being judgmental. We all experience things in life, sometimes similar things but we respond differently. For example, you may go through something and just lay and watch tv, or pray where the next person may overeat. Coping is different for every person. Addictions are little leeches. Leeches are parasites that sucks the blood out of you. Addictions not only suck the energy out of the people who are addicted but their people who are around them who want them better. Giving support can be exhausting, but imagine being the person who's addicted. They want to be better but when they look in the mirror, all they see is their scars from where the leech has caused satisfaction. This can cause the relapse of an addict. We all have a scar that tells a story. Some scars are visible for others to see and some are tucked away in a lock box because they're ashamed of the experience. Understanding and assisting anyone with an addiction is a hard task which requires patience. You're not the healer of the universe, you're only their support so stop getting frustrated.

You have a choice to walk around as a Scarred Person or an Overcomer.

1. A scarred person makes excuses for their negative behavior and always responds defensively.

2. An overcomer is not afraid to be light unto the world and sharing their story to help others. They respond compassionately.

Stop saying I'm not going to teach people how to love me. I've got bad news for you!

You will for the rest of your life! You will teach people what words mean when it comes to your feelings so that you can establish those boundaries. Understanding boundaries is a part of respect. Love is not just an emotion, but it's action. If they respect them then they're honored to be in your life if they don't; Guess what? You don't need them in your life and that's a choice they make. Always remember love is what love does. If they're not willing to love you unconditionally as it's reciprocated this is not a relationship you want in your life. I prefer not to have relationships with people that can't take accountability for their actions. When your apology is not just words, but changed behavior, then we can work something out. You're not for everyone.

"When your intentions are pure, you don't lose anyone, they lose you." ~ Nipsey Hussle

Addictions are only really acknowledged when it's drugs and secondly food. What are some things that you're addicted to that do not serve you or bring you full joy and peace?

_____

_____

_____

_____

_____

_____

_____

_____

Chapter 9

Community

Growing up, I remember people saying it takes a village to raise a child. The community was full of hate, love, scandals and violence. When it came to the children, the dysfunction became functional. However, so many things were missed. Many children who are now adults were sexually assaulted by family members or friends of the family. Neglected by their guardians because they were either chasing money, men, women, Jesus or on drugs. The kids are now adults trying to adult with unhealed childhood traumas. Children expect adults to know what they're doing when it comes to raising them but the adults who are raising children are children in adult bodies who are trying to figure it out as they go. There is no handbook to parenting, that's why a community is needed to help influence youth to make better decisions.

How can mental illness be assisted in the community and workplace? The past few years mental illness has really been in the spotlight because of killings and suicides as if it's something new. Being mentally conscious is not a trend but a battle real people struggle with daily. Experiences in a person's life can cause mental illness; you're not just born with it all the time. There are some mental illnesses that people are born with out of their control and some come from traumatic experiences.

One unique thing about us is we all were created differently; Your brain, your fingerprint, the way you look is different from the next person. You may have similarities but no one is the same. Your perspective on life can be something that was instilled in you as a child to help formulate your thinking but it's up to you to broaden your thinking and Do your own research. I have noticed things and ways I was taught; I don't teach my child. Not saying I was taught wrong but I was taught a learned behavior from another teacher. But the great thing about this life, as you get older and mature you learn your own perspective. It's ok to agree to disagree with others and not be mad. It's not about who is right or wrong. I respect you and expect the same. I thank God everyday for making us different. If we were the same this world would be even more crazy. It's important that you acknowledge your truths. We all need someone in life. This life is to be shared with people who genuinely care for you.

To show love in the community doesn't require you to be a full activist but to just treat people like humans.

I learned as I continued to mask the pain. No one knew my struggles and I allowed them to misuse and abuse me in many ways. I was treating people how I desired to be loved but had never experienced the love I was displaying.

Although my light was dimmed because of my own circumstances, it was never out. I was able to shine enough for others to feel love. Always remember, someone is always doing worse than you. A simple smile could change their day. In life you're reaping your harvest means enjoying what you worked hard for, going through the sowing stage and the storm is raging or just coming out of a storm and waiting for your harvest to manifest. You will experience some time of loss whether it's mental, physical, financially or socially. You may think your neighbor is ok because of the way they dress and because of what they drive, because they've become a master of masking their pain. It takes a village to exemplify what love is. We must act on it. Pour into the children around you because this new generation is lost and have not experienced true love from their parents because we grew up on a grind to be better than our parents, So, they lack social skills and fundamentals of building healthy relationships because they want to be loved. Choosing to be 'loved' within your community requires transparency and no judgment within. People are so guarded because of the hate in the world. However, it's up to us as individuals to lead the way positively. The universe is designed for us to need each other. We weren't created to be alone. You can make a difference if you desire to do so. If you don't desire to make a difference, at least desire to be loved by accepting the fact that we're all different but we can live life together in peace.

Remember you are what you attract. If you want to be light, surround yourself with people who have light.

Your healing is also driven by the people who you surround yourself with. Have people who understand your boundaries. Have relationships with people who inspire and challenge your thinking to be better. Most importantly, have relationships with people who will hold you accountable.

Your circle should be a balance and replication of the character you have or desire to be.

Ask yourself, how are you impacting your community with simply Showing love? Is your circle serving you in the proper capacity that you need to be healthy?

_____

_____

Chapter 10

Don't suffer in silence. Depression is the number one silent killer. Depression starts with your brain then attacks your body. It can cause body aches, lower your immune system, cause things like seizures, high blood pressure, diabetes and many more things to attack your body. Depression will have you pretending to be happy until you've had enough. It will make you feel alone, and lost at the same time. You may have a support system so you question why you feel sad but no one is present.

You can get through anything in life as long as you maintain a positive attitude. Will it be moments that are unbearable? Heck yea! But your attitude and mindset will help your end result. If you feel like you can't do it? You won't! If you feel like I can do it but I know it will be hard but I'm not giving up. You will Conquer the world. Your mindset has to be shifted.

Tips to be free because depression can hit you like a ton of bricks at any day and time. Understanding how to cope allows you to deal with your emotions.

Well, how do I deal with my emotions if they're all over the place?

First, You will feel!!!

Allow yourself a moment to cry, sit and feel whatever you're feeling. This is giving yourself grace to be human. We often just go through things and move on to the next thing while life is just kicking us in the ass. Then boom we're mentally exhausted and feel alone because mentally you've alienated yourself to just take blow after blow with no outlet.

2. Discuss what you're feeling with someone you trust who will show you love is what love does. Stop sharing your business with people who don't know what love is.

3. If you're still feeling down because those methods may not have brought you peace yet write, down what's bothering you. Remember you're not alone. Start living in the present. Realize what you deserve. Allow your light in you to shine; even if you feel it's dim to lead your way. Write down what you feel is blocking you from moving forward.

Once you're done, rip it and or burn it. Give it back to the Universe and ask that it be removed from your thoughts. Ask for a covering of your ancestors to protect you. It's not a special way to talk to God of the universe because he knows all things; just release and give it to him. We hold on to things because we expect people to respond or act how we want them to act. When choosing peace and understanding that life is more simple just being happy you can accomplish a lot of things if you just choose love.

A simple adult conversation can illuminate a lot of childish misunderstandings if people start taking accountability. Every action is a reaction. Never stop being you, even if people don't like it. Understand that jealousy can be hidden in compliments. People will laugh in your face, praise you while envying you.

Love and support but they hate and envy you. Always watch the energy that's around you, You are loved! Your anxiety will tell you the wrong thing. So keep your mind free of negative thoughts. You are amazing, kind, smart, beautiful and you matter more than you know. You're not a failure. A failure is a person who doesn't complete a task. Having detours is ok as long as you keep the pace. You're strong, healing comes with time. Stop seeking perfection. You glow differently when you're not hating, hurting, self-sabotaging, bitter, messy or vindictive. When choosing to let things be that are out of your control is a different type of peace. It will open airways for higher frequency by releasing anything that has been blocking you to be great and to manifest what's meant for you.

Until you prioritize your healing; you will attract people that will wound you again. Stop giving people satisfaction over your life and thoughts. Your scars are a replication of your battle And a reminder of you to know how far you've come. Choose to be a light to your path, not just others. Healing from your trauma will require you to unlearn behavior you thought was just normal or ok. Always remember love is what love does. People use the word so lightly forgetting how simple yet heavy it can be. I love you but, are my actions love? Is my action pulling the weight that my mouth speaks?

Don't expect love if you're not requiring yourself to do the same. As you're building a stronger relationship with yourself, the people that are meant to be a part of your life will be. You will attract how you treat yourself. Your light is going to irritate unhealed people.

When you display some sort of darkness; it will find you. As soon as you authentically become light you will receive light and everyone around you will have your best interest at heart. You will see the leeches peeping through a mile away because you got out of your own head and chose to live intentionally on purpose.

Everyday set intentions for yourself to be a better you than the day before. You deserve it. Remember that you're more than enough!! Hug yourself, encourage yourself. Love on YOU as if you would love on someone else in need. You're a magical being. As long as you believe it. Don't be a walking time bomb. Live in the present.

There will be obstacles such as traffic jams or a simple disagreement that could alter your mood at that moment. Don't sit in that. Take a deep breath and still conquer the day. If you fall short, guess what? No one is perfect. Try again the next day.

You will feel like you're going through hell and fighting with the enemy everyday. Don't quit. The power of the tongue is a strong force but when your tongue aligns with your thoughts; trust me you would be a force to be reckoned with. Winning in life is not a competition with people but a competition with self. Stop thinking and comparing yourself to other people because you have the same magic as they do, if you believe in yourself.

Take this time to let it go...

_____

_____

_____

_____

_____

_____

Love is what love does. Are you intentionally loving the people around you but more importantly YOURSELF?

_____

_____

_____

_____

_____

_____

_____

_____

Chapter 11

I've been knocked down a million times. I have grieved both parents in different aspects, over family and friends. I've been homeless. I know what it's like to go to school, get a master's degree and not get the dream job. Not because I'm not qualified but because no one wants to give me a chance. That in itself is a hard pill to swallow applying to over 300 jobs in state and out state within a three-month period and 1000's over the years. I have experience but no one has really given me a call back. To have degrees and get entry level pay. Struggling to pay my bills and to provide for my child with inconsistent help. My self-esteem was shot. I know what it's like to be in a relationship and not feel wanted. I know what it's like to give your all in a relationship and still get cheated on. I know what it's like to pour your love out to people who just listen but their ego is not willing to respect your feelings. I know what it's like to have friends who just don't get you. Rejection can put you so low where you feel like you're not enough. I know what it's like to feel like the odd ball in the family. I know what it's like to just feel alone in the world. To say all of this and will still walk around with a smile but my inside was gray. Part of me believed and part of me was like I'm over this. I still continued to be the "people pleaser" and give into relationships that didn't reciprocate the unconditional love I gave. I lost friendships because I didn't know how to properly communicate my feelings because of the dysfunction I was used to. I didn't trust anyone with my feelings. I was so used to disappointments that I started to just disappoint myself. I started to carry the weight of the NO''s. Carrying the weight of just obstacles because everything has hit me. I was broken for years healing people while encouraging and uplifting them through their brokenness.

They didn't know that I was being fueled by their wins. They didn't know I was acting like I was healed but healing as I was being called to be the healer. Not one time did I get envious or jealous over others successes. However, I did question why not me? It was my purpose Through my gift to heal others; I knew that I was enough. I knew I didn't bring things to the table but I brought the whole table and the chairs so I can protect my peace and know who's sitting there with me. But why wasn't my success not lucrative financially? Then boom!! Spirit said, are you homeless? I said No. Can you get in your car and go? I said yes! Can you provide for your child? I said yes! Are y'all healthy? I said yes! When I started to remember who I was and know who I was becoming and looked over my life finding solitude in just being grateful brought a different type of peace over my life. Those coals started to light me up more. As long as I pursue the passion that was given to me I will never go without again. God will always cover me. I used to sing a song to myself to get me through.

Song by Milton Brunson and The Thompson Community Singers

"The race is not given, to the swift nor to the strong,

But to the one that endures, until the end,

They'll be problems,

And sometimes you will walk alone, but I know, that I know that I know,

It will work out, yes it will for the good of them

Eyes have not seen, and neither have ears heard,

The things that God has prepared for them,

For, for, for them

Sometimes, you may have to cry,

And sometimes, you may have to may have to moan

But I know, that I know, that I know,

Things will work out, yes they will,

For the good of them"

This song still gets me through rough times and helps me remember who I am.

I am a diamond in the rough. The heat and pressure used to make me who I am; I need to honor my struggles. I will not disrespect myself any longer by allowing others to devalue me. I will not resent people for mishandling me. I will forgive myself and them for not loving me enough to handle me with care while respecting me. I can't give the love I desire to people but I'm not willing to love myself. I forgive ME!! I will love myself properly. I will treat my temple well. I will date myself. I will spend one on one time with myself to be refreshed. In order for me to be good to others I must be good to myself.

I also know that this is not the end for me or the end for you. I know it's so cliche to say that God has you. That's the typical response. Always remember to have yourself! Know you are ENOUGH! The creator of the universe and your ancestors will help you along your path as long as you believe.

Believe in yourself emotionally, physically and mentally. Darkness does not last forever. All of my 'no's are coals to the fire that's inside of me. Every No I get is just another coal to keep my fire going.

I hope this book encourages you to help YOU. Don't give up. Always remember love is what love does. Love is an unconditional feeling. Don't allow the slowness of your journey to make you envious of others who get to their destinations faster. Love you despite your flaws and how you treat you. You will feel tired and exhausted; that's ok. You will shed tears. I can't tell you how many times I've cried. That's ok! You will lose relationships. Everyone is not going to be proud of you and everyone is not meant to go with you. That's absolutely ok! As a matter of fact, this is the part that brings a little pain when it happens. Everyone is not going to understand your level of maturity or growth and that's ok. Keep pushing and fighting for your victory. Every single person you lose along the way will be replaced with people who really value you.

To win you must be ready to train. Training involves a process. The weight may get heavy. You may feel drained but every day you will see results slowly.

Sometimes you may feel as if you hit a plateau, and nothing is changing or moving. Keep going!! Remember this, it's ok to avoid certain people for your mental health. It's not weakness, it's wisdom because you're putting yourself first. Don't allow others to dump their shit on you. Their shit could be insecurities, emotional, manipulative and abusive traumas. Remember don't compare yourself to others. Some people will never tell you what they're going through. Not everyone will have food on the table, loving parents, a change of clothes daily, a loving spouse, good friends or someone to talk to. Most people mask their struggle with a smile.

So do me a favor and don't compare yourself to others because you don't know their struggles. "Faking it until you make it" is real so you will never know who's struggling because they've mastered masking to look good.

Set intentions every day to follow the steps listed below to guide you through your journey. Don't fear starting over, try new things to step into your destiny.

1. Focus on you. Love on you! You owe it to yourself to show up everyday for you to become closer to what you've dreamed of being.

2. Break the cycle of functioning broken. Our parents were traumatized, their parents, and their parent's parents were traumatized. It just keeps going until someone decides to break the cycle by reevaluating themselves for the sake of healing the family lineage.

3. Choose not to be broken, but heal inside out by processing your fears. Trust yourself!

4. Remember Manifestation is real. If you stay positive with your thoughts and speech, watch how things shift. I am my ancestors' wildest dream. What are you? Be a chain breaker for yourself.

5. Take accountability for your own actions along your journey. Don't allow anyone's ignorance to detour you from being your best SELF.

6. Have people around you who love on you, hold you accountable and elevate you.

7. Remember this; Forgiveness does not mean the pain instantly goes away. You just learn to heal from the lesson learned.

8. Always forgive yourself and others so that you don't block what's meant for you to manifest, through Trusting the process.

9. Learn who you really are by understanding what makes you 'YOU'. Do the shadow work by acknowledging your flaws. Digging deep to discover your whys. Your past does not define you but it is a part of you that has equipped you to function in the world. Trust yourself!!!

10. Clear your auras! Doing this releases internal blockages. We have 7 chakras; crown, third eye, throat, heart, solar plexus, sacral, and root chakra. When you're grounded, love yourself, you can receive love from others. When you take accountability, you're able to see situations beyond just your feelings, you're able to experience the joy and light in things rather than just seeing it at the surface level. You can communicate effectively without being defensive or coming off offensive. You're able to walk with confidence understanding your power by thinking practically.

11. Lastly, learn to live in the present (in the now). Don't think about the past or the future but live right now. Find gratitude in just surviving in that moment. I'm not saying not to have dreams. I'm saying don't dwell on them where you miss important moments or people in your life because time has passed you by.

_____

_____

_____

Every heartbreak and every loss contains its own seed, it's own lesson on how to improve your performance the next time. - Malcolm X

So master the lesson and sow those seeds. Then watch your harvest grow from the perseverance you had during those difficult times.

As you heal, you will develop the importance of having boundaries. This will be a daily reminder as people will assume you're still that person they used to mishandle. Identify what your boundaries are when communicating with people. Be at peace with choosing your happiness. Healing as you go through life, experiencing grief as you continue to dream, smile, be loved and give love is all a daily cycle. This is why it's important to protect your mental space because one of these can shift your whole world if you don't take care of yourself on a regular basis. You will learn what triggers you on your healing journey and that will tell you how to create boundaries as it assists you in showing you what you need to heal from.

It's important to listen to yourself; your own intuition when socializing with people who don't understand where you are mentally and along your journey. You sometimes have to interact with people in doses to protect your energy.

Write your boundaries down, acknowledge them within yourself so that you can address when they're crossed without responding with emotions, but being firm in how you would like to receive respect. You may categorize them by family, friends and work.

_____

_____

_____

_____

_____

_____

As this book has given many examples of how love can be deceiving or to find love. How can you become intentional with loving who you are? Start here! Write down things you love about you. Then on another page write down things you struggle with about you. The flaws, the ugly truth that you feel about yourself; Let's face them head on.

_____

_____

_____

_____

_____

_____

Now that you see both lists; the next step is to acknowledge them by working towards making your flaws flawless. This is a part of the process that keeps moving because you must start with a change of mindset. Once you change your thinking, then you can train your thoughts to be intentional. Instead of saying I'm not! You new thoughts are I am! Instead I can't! Your new thought is I can!

This book addresses how depression slipped in and tried to attack me for years. I became a walking zombie because of my lack of knowledge of knowing what depression was and the different types. Then once I became aware, the anxiety of going back would take a toll over my mental health. Life can be hard at times. Life can be great at times. Life can be overwhelming at times. Life can make you doubt yourself and the people around you at times.

God chose YOU to live your specific life and YOU to experience your journey.

You live it the best way YOU know and choose to become better everyday.

Your experience in this life is YOUR experience; don't let others tell You how to feel. Your feelings are YOURS.

Don't allow others to intimidate YOU from being YOU!

Don't let others stop you from living in your truth because they fear people will see them in a different way.

Live your life for YOU!

You are not alone. I can help you along your journey.

Visit me at:

www.realmcccoylife.com

God still loves you and so do I!! Sending you peace, love and light ~Jocelyn

Book cover design done by

J. Parker Designs

Email us: info@jparkerdesigns.org

Made in the USA
Columbia, SC
14 October 2021

46924320R00039